D1529895

Your Government:
How It Works

The U.S. Armed Forces

HILLSDALE PUBLIC LIBRARY
509 HILLSDALE AVE
HILLSDALE, N.J. 07642

Daniel E. Harmon

Arthur M. Schlesinger, jr.
Senior Consulting Editor

Chelsea House Publishers
Philadelphia

CHELSEA HOUSE PUBLISHERS

Production Manager Pamela Loos
Art Director Sara Davis
Director of Photography Judy L. Hasday
Managing Editor James D. Gallagher
Senior Production Editor J. Christopher Higgins

Staff for THE U.S. ARMED FORCES

Project Editor/Publishing Coordinator Jim McAvoy
Associate Art Director Takeshi Takahashi
Series Designers Takeshi Takahashi, Keith Trego

©2001 by Chelsea House Publishers, a subsidiary of Haights Cross
Communications. All rights reserved. Printed and bound in the
United States of America.

The Chelsea House World Wide Web address is
http://www.chelseahouse.com

First Printing
1 3 5 7 9 8 6 4 2

Library of Congress Cataloging-in-Publication Data

Harmon, Daniel E.
    The U.S. Armed Forces / Daniel Harmon.
        p. cm. — (Your government — how it works)
    Includes bibliographical references and index.
ISBN 0-7910-5994-4
    1. United States—Armed Forces—Juvenile literature. [1. United
States—Armed Forces—History.] I. Title. II. Series.

UA23 .H3643 2000
355'.00973—dc21   00-034594

Contents

Introduction

Government: Crises of Confidence

Arthur M. Schlesinger, jr.

FROM THE START, Americans have regarded their government with a mixture of reliance and mistrust. The men who founded the republic understood the importance of government. "If men were angels," observed the 51st Federalist Paper, "no government would be necessary." But men are not angels. Because human beings are subject to wicked as well as to noble impulses, government was deemed essential to assure freedom and order.

The American revolutionaries, however, also knew that government could become a source of injury and oppression. The men who gathered in Philadelphia in 1787 to write the Constitution therefore had two purposes in mind: They wanted to establish a strong central authority and to limit that central authority's capacity to abuse its power.

To prevent the abuse of power, the Founding Fathers wrote two basic principles into the Constitution. The principle of federalism divided power between the state governments and the central authority. The principle of the separation of powers subdivided the central authority itself into three branches—the executive, the legislative, and the judiciary—so that "each may be a check on the other."

YOUR GOVERNMENT: HOW IT WORKS examines some of the major parts of that central authority, the federal government. It explains how various officials, agencies, and departments operate and explores the political organizations that have grown up to serve the needs of government.

Introduction

The federal government as presented in the Constitution was more an idealistic construct than a practical administrative structure. It was barely functional when it came into being.

This was especially true of the executive branch. The Constitution did not describe the executive branch in any detail. After vesting executive power in the president, it assumed the existence of "executive departments" without specifying what these departments should be. Congress began defining their functions in 1789 by creating the Departments of State, Treasury, and War.

President Washington, assisted by Secretary of the Treasury Alexander Hamilton, equipped the infant republic with a working administrative structure. Congress also continued that process by creating more executive departments as they were needed.

Throughout the 19th century, the number of federal government workers increased at a consistently faster rate than did the population. Increasing concerns about the politicization of public service led to efforts—bitterly opposed by politicians—to reform it in the latter part of the century.

The 20th century saw considerable expansion of the federal establishment. More importantly, it saw growing impatience with bureaucracy in society as a whole.

The Great Depression during the 1930s confronted the nation with its greatest crisis since the Civil War. Under Franklin Roosevelt, the New Deal reshaped the federal government, assigning it a variety of new responsibilities and greatly expanding its regulatory functions. By 1940, the number of federal workers passed the 1 million mark.

Critics complained of big government and bureaucracy. Business owners resented federal regulation. Conservatives worried about the impact of paternalistic government on self-reliance, on community responsibility, and on economic and personal freedom.

When the United States entered World War II in 1941, government agencies focused their energies on supporting the war effort. By the end of World War II, federal civilian employment had risen to 3.8 million. With peace, the federal establishment declined to around 2 million in 1950. Then growth resumed, reaching 2.8 million by the 1980s.

A large part of this growth was the result of the national government assuming new functions such as: affirmative action in civil rights, environmental protection, and safety and health in the workplace.

Some critics became convinced that the national government was a steadily growing behemoth swallowing up the liberties of the people. The 1980s brought new intensity to the debate about government growth. Foes of Washington bureaucrats preferred local government, feeling it more responsive to popular needs.

But local government is characteristically the government of the locally powerful. Historically, the locally powerless have often won their human and constitutional rights by appealing to the national government. The national government has defended racial justice against local bigotry, upheld the Bill of Rights against local vigilantism, and protected natural resources from local greed. It has civilized industry and secured the rights of labor organizations. Had the states' rights creed prevailed, perhaps slavery would still exist in the United States.

Americans are still of two minds. When pollsters ask large, spacious questions—Do you think government has become too involved in your lives? Do you think government should stop regulating business?—a sizable majority opposes big government. But when asked specific questions about the practical work of government—Do you favor Social Security? Unemployment compensation? Medicare? Health and safety standards in factories? Environmental protection?—a sizable majority approves of intervention.

We do not like bureaucracy, but we cannot live without it. We need its genius for organizing the intricate details of our daily lives. Without bureaucracy, modern society would collapse. It would be impossible to run any of the large public and private organizations we depend on without bureaucracy's division of labor and hierarchy of authority. The challenge is to keep these necessary structures of our civilization flexible, efficient, and capable of innovation.

More than 200 years after the drafting of the Constitution, Americans still rely on government but also mistrust it. These attitudes continue to serve us well. What we mistrust, we are more likely to monitor. And government needs our constant attention if it is to avoid inefficiency, incompetence, and arbitrariness. Without our informed participation, it cannot serve us individually or help us as a people to attain the lofty goals of the Founding Fathers.

The Pentagon in Washington, D.C., is home to the country's Department of Defense. The vast majority of military functions originate from within this building.

CHAPTER

1

Our National Defense System

THE UNITED STATES IS the most powerful nation in the world, most journalists and historians agree. Since World War II, America has built and kept a strong **defense** system on land, at sea, and in the air. It consists of tens of thousands of weapons. But its most valuable resources are the millions of men and women who stand ready to defend American soil and American citizens and interests overseas.

The Nation's Early Years

After the American colonists won their independence from Britain more than two centuries ago, most of them did not believe we needed a regular army or navy. They thought the rest of the world would live peacefully with America.

They were wrong. American trading ships at sea became easy targets for pirates. They were also seized by European warships. Many

Widely accepted as one of the world's most advanced aircraft, the B-2 Stealth Bomber is just one small part of the United States armed forces. The United States armed forces are regarded as being the most powerful military presence on the face of the Earth.

U.S. seamen were "pressed" into service in the conquering ships' navies. The new republic needed a navy and marine force of its own. It also needed an army to protect frontier settlers as the country expanded westward.

When the country broke apart during its dreadful Civil War in 1861, both the North and the South raised formidable armies and navies. It was the century of the Industrial Revolution, the age of invention. America developed new weapons and tactics. After the war, its combined armed forces were in some ways the most advanced in the world.

Still, Americans were not inclined to keep a powerful army or navy during years of peace. In the 20th century, the country was drawn into two destructive world wars. Both times, our standing forces were weak, compared to those of other nations. We quickly had to enlist soldiers, sailors, and fliers and build warships, tanks, and planes.

The Modern Armed Forces

After the end of World War II, during the late 1940s, the United States government began to reorganize its military defense system. Russia—although it had been our **ally** during the last world war—declared its opposition to democracy, the American form of government. Russian leaders predicted there would someday be a great war between their Communist government and ours.

This raised many fears, not just in America but around the world. By then we had entered the atomic age. Awesome nuclear weapons were being built by both Russia and America—and later by smaller nations, as well. Soon, scientists estimated that the world had enough nuclear weapons to destroy all humankind.

Both sides knew that in order to prevent a nuclear war, they must contain trouble spots and resolve dangerous conflicts before they could grow into nuclear crises. To do that required constant vigilance and frequent intervention by "old-fashioned" military forces. America's leaders realized we needed an army, navy, and air force ready to fight and defend at a moment's notice. We also needed to keep pace with the Russian nuclear weapons **arsenal.**

Above all, we needed a central command system to coordinate and control our increasingly complex armed forces. The United States created a Joint Chiefs of Staff, made up of the highest officers of the United States Army, Navy, Air Force, and Marine Corps.

*Roman soldiers do battle with
the Huns at the gates of Rome.
In ancient times most wars were
fought in vicious combat using
swords, spears, and a variety of
other deadly weapons.*

CHAPTER

2

The Army

ARMIES ARE THE OLDEST type of armed force on Earth. In pre-historic times, primitive humans undoubtedly banded together as the need arose for protection or for hunting large and dangerous animals.

These were hardly "armies," as we know them—in fact, they were barely organized. But very early in human history, people learned the important lesson that there is strength in numbers.

Early Armies

As groups of people in different parts of the world began living in permanent villages and cities, they needed citizen-soldiers. These first armies were expected to protect their people from attack by others. If their people wanted to take over new land, their armies took it by force, if necessary.

It is believed that civilizations in the Middle East had armies more than 5,000 years ago. The Egyptians had armies at least 4,000 years ago. And by 500 B.C., the Chinese had produced a book on how warfare should be carried out.

These early armies consisted of professional soldiers who were paid to fight. They were highly trained. At first, they fought only with spears, knives, and bows and arrows. Soon, soldiers on horseback formed the first cavalry units. Two-wheeled, armored chariots were used with fearful effect by early military leaders like Alexander the Great.

More Armor and Power

The first soldiers wore little or nothing for protection. Soon, however, fighters were devising shields and helmets. Knights, professional soldiers in Europe during the Middle Ages, used heavy armor not only for themselves but for their horses.

Meanwhile, armies were increasing their firepower. By the 1300s, European armies were using crossbows—some of them so large they required several men to operate them. Then came the weapon that changed warfare forever: gunpowder.

Explosive powder had been used for centuries by the Chinese to produce spectacular fireworks. In the early 1300s, a German monk experimented with explosive weapons. By the time the Europeans began exploring and settling the Americas, they were using cannons and crude handheld firearms against whoever opposed them.

By the time of the American Revolution, Native Americans had acquired rifles from European traders and were using them in warfare along with their own traditional weapons: the tomahawk, bow and arrow, and spear.

America's First Army

When the American colonies declared their independence from England, one of the first acts of the Continental

Congress was to create a Continental army. This was done June 14, 1775. That made the army the first branch of the United States armed forces. Our navy was created shortly afterward, during the American Revolution. The U.S. Air Force did not come about until more than 170 years later.

George Washington was our army's first commander in chief. He led the Continental army through six years of hardship and uncertainty before the British finally surrendered. Washington later became the first president of the United States.

For 80 years after the Revolution, the U.S. Army was active not so much in defending the new nation but in helping it expand. During the first half of the 19th century, soldiers were sent to the frontier as it pushed further west. Their duties included mapping the new territories and ensuring the safety of American settlers. This led to confrontations with Native Americans throughout most of the 1800s. During the 1840s, the army was sent to the Southwest to fight the Mexicans over control of territories in what is today the southwestern United States.

The Civil War

All wars are terrible events. Few in history, though, have been as tragic as the American Civil War. In this war, Americans fought against other Americans. More than 200,000 died, and many more were wounded. For four years, from 1861 to 1865, America was gripped in its greatest national crisis.

The war began after 11 Southern states banded together to cut ties with the rest of the United States. They called themselves the Confederate States of America.

To President Abraham Lincoln and citizens of the North, this Southern "secession" was an act of rebellion. Unity had to be restored.

The nation's army officers were divided as war clouds gathered. Most officers from the Southern states chose to leave the United States Army and offer their military services to the Confederacy. Many officers on one side were good friends with officers on the other—but they found themselves fighting each other to the death.

In the end, the U.S. Army commanded by General Ulysses S. Grant defeated the main Confederate army commanded by General Robert E. Lee. The Confederacy was readmitted to the Union.

After the Civil War, many officers remained in the army and led the U.S. **Cavalry** in a bloody series of conflicts with the Indians in the West. The eventual result was that the Native Americans were confined to reservations, and their vast lands were occupied by white settlers.

The World Wars

World War I began in Europe in 1914. The United States tried to be neutral, taking neither the side of Germany nor of England and France. In 1917, however, American ships were sunk by the Germans, and the United States declared war against Germany. The war ended less than two years later, but by then more than 50,000 American soldiers and army airmen had been killed.

World War II began in 1939 when Germany took over some of its neighboring countries. Again, England and France were united in their fight against Germany and its allies (friendly nations). And again, the United States tried to stay out of the war.

In late 1941, though, Japan—one of Germany's allies—bombed the U.S. naval base at Pearl Harbor in Hawaii. Once more, America was involved in a world conflict.

This war cost the U.S. Army almost 300,000 lives—more than six times the number of army deaths in the First World War—before it ended in 1945. But again, America and its allies were victorious.

Recent Conflicts

Since World War II, American soldiers have fought in several wars. In the Korean War during the early 1950s, America helped South Korea defend itself from invasion by North Korea. This was the first full-scale war between the forces of democracy (championed by the United States) and the forces of Communism (championed by the Soviet Union). The conflict eventually ended in a "stalemate," or draw.

A few years later, the United States began sending advisers and, eventually, combat forces to South Vietnam in the Far East. This country was under attack by its Communist neighbor, North Vietnam. After many years of fighting, American soldiers gradually withdrew. America left the defense of South Vietnam to the South Vietnamese Army. Within a few years, South Vietnam was overrun by its enemy to the North.

America did not actually "lose" the Vietnam War. Because America withdrew, however, many people see the Vietnam War as a military humiliation or embarrassment.

In 1991, the U.S. armed forces went to the aid of another small country in distress. Kuwait in the Middle East was overpowered and occupied by its neighbor Iraq. Working with several allied countries, the United States quickly drove Iraqi forces out of Kuwait.

Today's Army

The U.S. Army now, like armies in days of old, is responsible for most of our military operations on land. It must be constantly ready to defend the country and, if necessary, to attack on enemy soil.

About 500,000 active-duty (full-time) men and women make up the U.S. Army today. Almost a million more serve in the army reserves or National Guard and as nonuniformed civilians who work for the army.

The Department of the Army is one branch of the U.S. Department of Defense. Its headquarters is in Washington, D.C., but major army units are based around the world. For example, the Eighth Army has its headquarters in South Korea. The U.S. Army, Europe, is based in Germany.

Joining the Army

Service in today's army (as in the other branches of our armed forces) is voluntary. Young men and women aren't required to join; they join only if they want to. To join voluntarily is called to enlist.

It hasn't always been that way. In times of war, the government usually has to use the military draft system. This requires able-bodied young people to serve in the armed forces. They can choose which branch they wish to serve; if they don't join the navy, air force, marines, Coast Guard, or a reserve force, then they are drafted into the U.S. Army.

The draft has been used in Europe and elsewhere for centuries. The Roman Empire required military service as early as 200 B.C. This requirement, called *conscription,* first was used in America during the Civil War. It was used again in World Wars I and II.

During the Vietnam War, a form of the draft called a *draft lottery* was created. Numbers were drawn at random for each day of the year. The number assigned to a person's birthday became his draft lottery number. December 6, for example, is the 340th day of the year—but it was the 10th date to be drawn in the lottery. Thus, if you were born on December 6, your draft lottery number was 10.

That meant you probably would be drafted. The army began drafting the number of young men it needed for the war effort, beginning with all those who had birthdays on lottery day 1. It then went to those who had birthday number 2, then 3, etc., until it had as many draftees as it needed.

In peacetime, when there is no draft, men and women ages 17–29 can apply for acceptance into the army. **Recruiting** offices are found in all major cities and even in many towns. There, the applicants take tests to determine whether they qualify for service and what types of skills they possess.

The modern army tries to use people in the areas in which they're especially gifted. In an earlier time, if you were interested in literature or health care or teaching or law or chemistry, you might find yourself in a totally different—and unappealing—army job. Today, however, the army tries to place you in a position in which you are likely to rapidly learn, develop, and excel.

An exhausted soldier lies prone in the mud during exercises at boot camp. Boot camp is a period of rigorous training in which enlistees develop many of the skills and the discipline they'll need to succeed in the military.

Army Training

Basic training camps are the dreaded places where enlistees (new recruits) in all branches of the service learn to become military personnel. At boot camp enlistees are given identical uniforms, and their hair is cut very short.

Rising early each morning, recruits undergo long days of physical exercise and drills. They receive instruction in weapon use, first aid, navigation or orienteering (finding one's way), and other essential skills they'll need. They learn the importance of taking orders and working as a team.

Boot camp in the army lasts eight weeks. Then the recruits are sent to special training schools where they will learn to perform their individual tasks in the army. These courses may take several weeks or several months.

When training is complete, soldiers begin service in their specialty area. More than 600 different kinds of jobs are offered by the U.S. Army today.

Regular soldiers begin service with the rank of private. They may be promoted to private first class, then corporal, then sergeant. The highest rank an enlisted man or woman can reach is sergeant major.

Officer Training

The U.S. Army has had a special training academy for its officers since 1802—just 20 years after the War of Independence. This is West Point in New York, located on the Hudson River, not far from New York City. Officially, it is known as the United States Military Academy. Commonly, we simply call it "West Point."

A military academy is very similar to a college—but its special purpose is to train people for national defense. Thousands of young people apply for admission to West Point every year; only a small fraction can be selected. They are nominated by their senators or congressional representatives. To be considered for West Point, most of them must rank in the top 10 percent of their high school classes in test scores and pass a physical examination.

Those who are chosen must undergo basic training just like non-officer enlistees. Then they begin four years of study, much like college students—but they follow military rules and customs each day and participate in regular drills and exercises. They graduate with a bachelor's degree in one of about 20 different study areas, or majors.

Between terms, the officer candidates undergo advanced military training. If they are going to lead soldiers in the field, they must be trained and tested. They must fully understand what they are doing and why. They must know how to handle any emergencies that might arise during a combat mission.

West Point students, called cadets, are actually employees of the army even while they are students. The government pays for their room, uniforms, and meals, as well as a small salary. In return, cadets commit themselves to at least six years of service in the army after graduation.

Students also may become army officers after completing army ROTC (Reserve Officer Training Corps) programs at ordinary colleges and universities. Or they may be accepted into Officer Candidate School (OCS).

After graduation, a new officer is commissioned as a second lieutenant in the U.S. Army. During his or her career, the officer may rise through the ranks to become a first lieutenant, captain, major, colonel, and—at the top of the command chain—general.

Certain types of professional **civilians** with skills the army needs—most notably doctors—may be given "direct commissions." That is, they may be commissioned as officers without having to go through regular officer training programs (although some military training is still required).

Different Types of Soldiers

Trained soldiers might be assigned to one of many kinds of army units:

★ *Infantry*. These are the kinds of soldiers we usually think of when we think of the army. Usually operating in groups, they use rifles, pistols, grenades, and other small weapons to defend land areas or, if necessary, to capture new territory and hold it.

A wave of Blackhawk helicopters deploy members of the army's Special Forces during Operation Desert Storm in Saudi Arabia. The combined efforts of each particular unit of the U.S. Army are essential to their success in any operation.

★ *Artillery.* These individuals operate heavy weapons and equipment, including huge guns called howitzers. Howitzers can fire powerful explosive shells at distances of more than 10 miles. The army **artillery** includes rocket-fired weapons.

★ *Armored Units.* Tanks are the most common armored weapons. They are extremely high-powered—but also mobile. They can move quickly, even while fighting. Heavily protected by armor plates, they can fire explosives up to three miles.

★ *Missile Units*. Using both nuclear and traditional explosives, some army missiles have a range of more than 1,000 miles. They can be used to attack enemy locations far away or to shoot down enemy aircraft.

★ *Aircraft*. Army airplanes and helicopters are used both for transporting soldiers and for supporting them with firepower from the air.

★ *Special Forces*. Green Berets and rangers are highly trained for special—often highly dangerous—operations such as guerrilla warfare and survival. They may be sent to fight behind enemy lines, often for long periods of time. This may require them to learn foreign languages and customs in order to operate effectively.

Besides combat units like those above, the army needs combat support soldiers. These include engineers (for designing and building bridges and other structures), military police, and chaplains (spiritual leaders). They also include Signal Corps specialists who set up and operate radio, phone, and other forms of communication.

The army also uses combat service support soldiers. These men and women provide transportation, medical services, and legal services. They also manage the army's payroll, making sure all soldiers are paid on schedule.

With new technology, today's soldiers are working not only with guns, howitzers, and missiles, but with computers and satellites. Ground soldiers and aircraft crews can use special eye goggles that let them see at night. Other forms of technology are just as amazing. The army is constantly changing and improving.

Our army once was a ragtag band of men bearing crude, unreliable muskets. Now it is a highly trained organization of men and women using space-age weapons and equipment. Each year brings new changes. The army someone joins 10 years from now will be quite different from—and much more powerful than—the army today.

The Harry S. Truman, *the United States' most technologically advanced aircraft carrier, is seen here during its construction as it is moved to a mooring by a tugboat. The United States Navy has fleets located in most major bodies of water.*

CHAPTER 3

The Navy

IN ALL THE WORLD'S oceans, thousands of United States Navy vessels are constantly on patrol. They are responsible for protecting the country's interests at home and in foreign nations.

The navy has major fleets in the Atlantic and Pacific Oceans. These fleets are divided into forces that patrol large bodies of water. The Atlantic Fleet, for example, includes the Sixth Fleet, which patrols the Mediterranean Sea.

Navy ships are of every type. They include gigantic aircraft carriers—actual air bases that can be moved quickly to any area of the globe. Fighting ships are equipped not just with heavy guns and other types of weapons but also with highly complicated communication and detection equipment. They are joined by supply and repair ships, minesweepers, research vessels, hospital ships, small but fast hydrofoil patrol craft, tugboats (used to maneuver large vessels in close quarters to or near ports) and other kinds of vessels.

Meanwhile, invisible below the surface of the ocean are deadly submarines that can launch powerful torpedoes and even nuclear missiles at enemy targets. Overhead, the navy keeps watchful eyes on our watery planet.

Early Navies

Nations have used ships to carry people and cargo since ancient times. Sadly, they also have fought one another since ancient times. In their fights to control the seas and shipping, they quickly devised ships of war.

Early navies consisted simply of armed soldiers aboard boats and ships. There were no missiles or heavy guns or torpedoes. In order to fight, the vessels had to draw alongside each other. Then the soldiers fought hand-to-hand with spears, swords, and bows and arrows, trying to board and capture the enemy ship.

Gunpowder began to be used during the 1300s and 1400s. Since then ships have carried monstrous cannons. Cannons could fire powerful explosives across the water at other ships or at fortresses on shore hundreds of yards—and eventually, miles—away. The nature of naval warfare thus changed. Modern warships aren't as concerned with having their sailors board an enemy ship as they are with sinking the enemy vessel or at least putting it out of action.

National leaders found that by building fleets of powerful gunships, they could dominate foreign ports and shipping. At the same time, they could defend their own ports and merchant ships. They could capture enemy cargo vessels. The country that controlled the sea also controlled much of what happened on land.

The Birth of the United States Navy

When our Continental Congress set about to prepare the colonies for the War of Independence against England, it first established a Continental army. Then it created a Continental navy. This was in 1775. In 1798, long after the Revolutionary War was over, Congress established the official United States Navy.

Captain John Paul Jones fights the British from the deck of the Bonhomme Richard *during the Revolutionary War.*

About 60 ships served America during the Revolution. Our most famous naval hero of that war was Captain John Paul Jones. In a smoky, bloody battle, his ship *Bonhomme Richard* captured the British ship *Serapis*. In the thick of the fighting, with his own vessel heavily damaged, Jones shouted his famous words, "I have not yet begun to fight!"

During the 1790s, the navy built up a new sailing fleet. It was led by three large, fast ships called frigates. These ships—the *Constitution* ("Old Ironsides"), *Constellation,* and *United States*—became three of our most famous naval vessels. The *Constitution* has been restored and can be seen dockside today in Boston, Massachusetts. The *Constellation* sailed for a century and a half. Also restored, it can be visited today in Baltimore, Maryland.

From Sail to Steam

By the time of the Civil War (1861–65), more and more ships were being powered by steam engines that turned propeller shafts. For many years, they continued to use sails, too. Eventually, however, most oceangoing vessels abandoned sail power.

Two of the first sail-less ships were the Union's *Monitor* and the Confederacy's *Merrimac*. These two strange "ironclad" vessels fought each other in the harbor near Newport News, Virginia, in 1862.

The Merrimac *and the* Monitor *do battle during the American Civil War. Ironclad vessels such as these first appeared during the Civil War and have since evolved into the giant battleships and carriers which form the U.S. fleet today.*

The primary role of the U.S. Navy in the Civil War was to "blockade" the Southern ports of the Confederate States of America. Union ships stationed just outside these ports prevented ships from bringing supplies to the Confederacy.

Confederates built iron-sided vessels like the *Merrimac* in an effort to break through the blockade. By using ironclads themselves, U.S. Navy commanders were able to ward off the *Merrimac* and similar ships.

Thus, the Civil War was a major turning point in the development of the navy. This era proved the value of both steam power and armored plating aboard warships. In just a short time, America's navy would consist almost totally of metal-plated, steam-powered vessels.

The 20th Century Navy

When America entered World War I in 1917, the navies of the world believed a ship's greatest strength was size. Big ships firing big guns were the pride of a country's fleet. (They also were the prime targets of enemy nations.)

These were the battleships. Until World War II (1939–45), a navy's strength was measured in large part

HILLSDALE PUBLIC LIBRARY
509 HILLSDALE AVE
HILLSDALE, N.J. 07642

by the number and size of its great battleships. Germany became the battleship leader with famous monsters like the *Bismarck* and *Tirpitz*.

Two things changed the way naval leaders thought about battleships, heavy cruisers, and other large ships. One was the improvement of the submarine. These small underwater craft could take down a mighty battleship with a surpise attack using torpedoes. The other factor was the improvement of warplanes. Navy airplanes not only could sweep a ship's decks with machine-gun bullets; they also could drop torpedoes from the sky.

In fact, the act that infuriated America and brought it into World War II was a large-scale attack by enemy airplanes. Japanese pilots took off from aircraft carriers in the Pacific Ocean near Hawaii. Striking by surprise early on December 7, 1941, they almost totally destroyed America's Pacific fleet anchored at Pearl Harbor.

The U.S. Navy used battleships, large cruisers, and smaller, fast destroyers in World War II. It still uses these types of ships today. Increasingly, though, it began to rely more on submarine power and on the massive aircraft carrier with its fighting planes. The first American aircraft carrier was the *Langley*, which went to sea in 1922.

A few years after World War II ended, the U.S. Navy began building submarines and other types of ships powered by nuclear ("atomic") engines. The first, the atomic submarine *Nautilus*, amazed the world when it traveled under the Arctic ice pack all the way from the Pacific Ocean to the Atlantic in 1958!

Nuclear submarines do not have to surface for refueling very often. That means they can stay on patrol for months—remaining underwater almost the whole time.

During the Korean War in the early 1950s and the Vietnam War and Persian Gulf War much later, U.S. naval vessels supported ground troops. They transported equipment and soldiers and directed heavy artillery fire at enemy shore locations. Navy pilots flew dangerous combat missions over sea and land.

The Navy Today

Navy ships today range from small patrol vessels to enormous aircraft carriers. The carrier *Harry S. Truman* is almost 1,100 feet long. It supports 90 planes and helicopters. More than 5,000 men and women make up its crew. It is literally a floating city that can be sent to distant shores and remain at sea for many months.

Cruisers, armed with guns, missiles, and torpedoes, are not nearly as large as carriers. But they are powerful and fast, traveling more than 30 mph (miles per hour) at sea. A cruiser has a crew of several hundred sailors.

Modern submarines are surprisingly fast, too. The newer ones can travel more than 25 mph on the surface. But most of the time they are out of sight, beneath the surface, sometimes hundreds of feet down. They can fire torpedoes and missiles underwater.

Hundreds of jobs are open in navy service. In the old days, all workers were called "sailors" because almost everyone aboard a ship had to know how to climb aloft to take in or let out the heavy sails. Today's naval crews still are called sailors. But there are no sails to handle anymore. Instead, sailors perform a variety of tasks requiring special skills and training. Here are just a few:

★ *Mechanics* make sure the ship's engines operate smoothly. Aircraft mechanics also are needed on carriers and other ships that carry helicopters.

★ *Gunners* or "gunner's mates," know not only how to fire ships' guns and missiles, but how to fix them at sea and keep them constantly ready for use.

★ *Communications specialists* operate sophisticated radios and/or radar, SONAR (*sound navigation ranging*) and satellite equipment.

★ *Navigators,* using state-of-the-art equipment, can tell exactly where they are, where they are heading, and how long it will take their ship to get from one point to another.

★ *Airplane and helicopter pilots and crew members* pilot navy planes such as the Tomcat and Hornet that fly faster than the speed of sound. Some planes can fire guns, drop bombs, and/or launch small missiles. Navy helicopters may be used to track and bomb enemy submarines or, in peacetime, to perform search, rescue, and recovery operations.

Like the army's Green Berets, the navy has its own special force called SEALs (for *Sea, Air* and *Land*). News documentaries and movies made the SEALs popular among young people in the 1990s. Their work seems exciting and glamorous—but it is extremely dangerous. SEALs are rigorously trained for close combat, often behind enemy lines.

The navy today consists of almost 400,000 full-time sailors and officers. They are backed by more than 300,000 navy reservists.

Joining the Navy

Navy recruits must be 17–34 years old and in good health. They sign up for terms of four or six years. During that time, they may be assigned to ships. In that case, they may see much of the world—but they must get used to living long periods in cramped quarters. Some sailors receive assignments at shore bases and rarely go to sea, except for periodic training exercises.

Upon joining, "seaman recruits" (also called "boots") are sent to basic training much like the army's enlistees. The navy's basic training camp is called boot camp because in times past, sailors wore leggings on their ankles and calves that resembled boots.

A navy SEAL looks out from behind his camouflaged face paint during the war in Vietnam. The navy SEALs are one of the world's most highly trained close-combat units.

At boot camp, strenuous physical exercise gets trainees in excellent physical shape. They learn military drills and discipline. Training in modern seamanship gives them a variety of skills, from rope tying to survival at sea.

After basic training, seaman recruits are ranked *seaman apprentices*. They go to advanced schools to learn how to perform the specific jobs they will have in the navy. Jobs may include engine mechanics, electronics, gunnery, military law enforcement, military cooking, or a number of other professions.

Navy enlistees then become regular *seamen*. Seaman classes, which determine how much a person is paid, are ranked by number; for example, E-6. Enlisted men and women cannot become officers (unless they obtain college degrees and undergo a lengthy period of officer training). However, they can rise to the rank of *petty officer*. The highest rank an enlisted man or woman can attain in the navy is master chief petty officer.

Navy Officers

The U.S. Naval Academy is located at Annapolis, Maryland, about an hour's drive from downtown Washington, D.C. It was started at the site of an army fort in 1845. Today it is the college-like campus where the Navy trains many of its officers over a four-year period.

Students there, who are nominated for the academy by their congressional representatives or senators, are called *midshipmen*. While students, they undergo training both as sailors and as officers. It is a difficult, strictly disciplined four years.

Midshipmen at the academy are paid a small salary by the navy. When they graduate, they will have earned a college degree and the officer's rank of ensign in the United States Navy. They are committed to serve in the navy for at least five years.

Over the course of their naval careers, officers may advance through the ranks of lieutenant, commander, and captain. The highest-ranking naval officers are admirals— the equivalent of generals in other service branches.

Men and women also may become navy officers by completing the navy's version of ROTC at a regular college. If they've already graduated from college when they become interested in a navy career, they may apply for Officer Candidate School (OCS). If accepted, they undergo 13 weeks of intensive training to become navy officers.

As in other service branches, ministers, doctors, lawyers, and other professionals may become naval officers with little training, compared to regular officers.

Navy careers are rewarding in many ways. Besides their salaries, sailors are provided with housing and meals or are paid extra to make their own living arrangements off-base. Submariners and flyers receive additional hazardous duty pay. Navy personnel and their families receive free medical care. After 20 years, a sailor can retire from the navy with retirement pay and benefits.

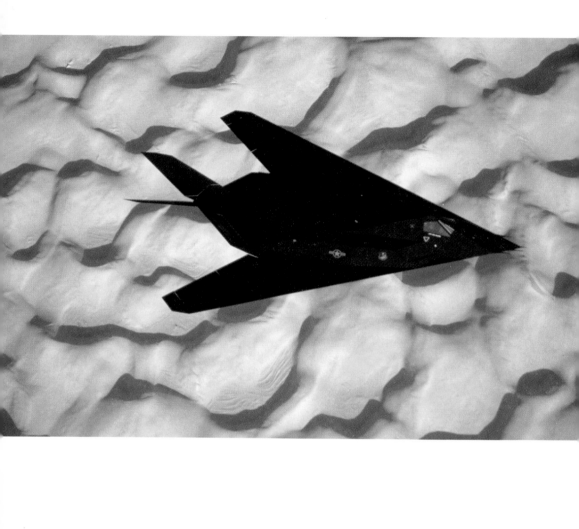

The F-117 Nighthawk stealth fighter is capable of avoiding radar due to the material from which it is constructed and its unique shape. It is believed by some that a variety of top secret aircraft which are more advanced than the F-117 are currently in use by the United States Air Force.

CHAPTER 4

The Air Force

AIR AND SPACE—THOSE are the domains of the United States Air Force (USAF). Even before the Wright brothers made their famous first airplane flight in 1903, many leaders knew that one day flight would be the key to military power. The nation that controlled the skies would become the strongest on Earth.

Most military historians agree the prediction was correct—and the United States, at this point in time, is believed to possess the best air force. The U.S. Air Force is well known for its incredibly fast and deadly fighters and bombers. But it also boasts state-of-the-art observation planes and cargo planes that can transport enormous amounts of goods—and people.

The air force also controls most of our country's arsenal of guided missiles. It has missiles that can shoot down other missiles, with no humans required to pilot them into "harm's way." These

Two F-16 fighters perform maneuvers high above the Earth. The weapons loaded aboard aircraft such as this can be fired and then guided by laser, making them extremely precise and accurate.

weapons can be launched and controlled from command bases hundreds and even thousands of miles away.

Russia also has a powerful air force. Russia was the main part of the Soviet Union, which was the United States' great rival after World War II (as discussed earlier). In 1991, when the Soviet Union was broken up into many smaller nations, Russia was the strongest of these new countries—and it became the chief concern of the U.S. Defense Department.

Before There Were Warplanes

How did America's amazing aerial might come to be?

The story of any country's air force must begin with the history of human flight. For thousands of years, people fantasized about the possibility of flight. What would it be like to fly like a bird? How might the Earth appear, looking down from the sky? What if one could travel freely over great distances, flying above rugged mountains, wide rivers, and other natural obstacles. It was a captivating idea.

The French were the first to fly. In June 1783—shortly after America won its War of Independence—two brothers named Montgolfier launched a hot-air balloon they had made out of silk and paper. They inflated it outdoors over an oven and watched it ascend until it was a tiny bulb high above them. They estimated the balloon reached an altitude of 6,000 feet—an incredible height for that time.

This balloon carried no pilot. It proved, however, that a manned flight was possible. Just four months later, another Frenchman named Jean François Pilâtre de Rozier went up in a balloon over Paris. For almost five minutes, he and his contraption floated in the air. Thus, Rozier is believed to have been the first human to fly.

Benjamin Franklin, the great American statesman who was living in France at that time, was fascinated by these balloon experiments. Already he was thinking of ways balloons could be used by armies.

Actually, the French immediately created an air force of sorts. In 1794, France was engaged in one of Europe's frequent wars of that era. The French military used balloonists to look down and observe enemy army movements located behind hills and other obstacles.

Almost 10 years later, the first manned balloon flight occurred in the United States. Rising from Philadelphia, Pennsylvania—the first American capital city—it stayed aloft for an astounding three-quarters of an hour. It finally settled to Earth in New Jersey farmland, 15 miles away. The pilot, not surprisingly, was another Frenchman, Jean-Pierre-François Blanchard.

For the next 70 years, balloon experiments became more common in America and Europe. In a conflict between the Austrians and the Italians in 1849, the Austrians sent unmanned balloons over the city of Venice bearing time bombs. Unhappily for the Austrians, the fickle winds above the city shifted direction. Some of the bombs exploded in Venice, and others wafted back behind Austrian lines before going off!

During the Civil War, the Union army created a balloon corps. The Confederates also used balloons. These balloons, manned by aerial scouts, would go straight up to a great height, tethered by long ropes to the ground. From there, the occupants could observe where the opposing army units were, several miles away, and in which direction (or directions) they were moving. This was a real improvement in army scouting because it showed the "big picture" all at once. And with specially rigged telegraph lines linking balloon and ground crews, the information could be sent quickly to headquarters below.

Aerial reconnaissance, or spying, was a dangerous assignment, though. As you can imagine, a manned balloon presented a very large target to enemy sharpshooters and even to artillerymen firing cannons!

Sprouting Wings

A number of Americans were trying to invent a controllable airplane by 1900. The ones who made the most famous names for themselves were Orville and Wilbur Wright, two brothers who made bicycles for a living in Dayton, Ohio.

The Wright brothers were not bumbling experimenters who chanced upon an airplane design that would work. They labored long hours over a period of years studying different wing shapes and other factors that affect flying.

After they settled on a basic design, they needed a safe, open place to test their work. They required a strong, constant wind to provide "lift" for the machine. The place they chose was the wide, sandy beach near Kitty Hawk on the Outer Banks of North Carolina.

The week before Christmas 1903, younger brother Orville won a coin toss and lay prone in the middle of their plane's lower wing. Powered by a small motor, the Wright plane had two long, broad wings braced one above the other—a "biplane." For 12 glorious seconds, Orville Wright was airborne . . . and moving!

During that first powered flight, Orville traveled only 120 feet. Imagine a football kickoff in which the return specialist carries the ball from the goal line to the 40-yard line before being tackled. That's a good kickoff return, but it isn't very far for an airplane to fly. Yet, it was a monumental step at the dawn of air travel and air combat.

A New Kind of War

The United States Air Force is only half a century old. The country went through both world wars in the 1900s without an official, separate air force. But we definitely had air power.

Developing effective airplanes for military use fell to our two long-standing armed forces branches, the army and navy. The army created a special Army Air Service. By the end of World War I (1918), our pilots were having a significant effect on the war effort.

In this war, they flew planes made of wooden frames covered with canvas. Today's automobiles can go faster than World War I planes could fly. Early bombs were simply sacks of explosives that the pilots or their companions tossed from open cockpits onto enemy troops or buildings. And the first air-to-air combat adventures, or "dogfights," were fought between opposing pilots shooting pistols at each other as they zigzagged through the sky.

Inventors soon figured out a way to time the firing of a lightweight machine gun with the turning of an airplane propeller. Thus, combat fliers could direct machine-gun fire straight ahead, through the large circle made by the propeller blades.

Thus arrived the age of the "ace" fighter pilots. Baron Manfred von Richthofen of Germany was clearly the best of his day; called the "Red Baron," he shot down 80 planes and military balloons. America's top ace, Eddie Rickenbacker, shot down 26 aircraft.

Meanwhile, the navy was experimenting with the use of ships as both launching pads and landing pads for airplanes. In 1922, the navy introduced the *Langley*, its first aircraft carrier. Just 20 years later, carriers would become recognized as the most important ships in a modern navy.

Mitchell Sounds the Alarm

Perhaps the man who did more than anyone else to promote a separate, powerful air force for the United States was Billy Mitchell. He was an army aviator who had seen air power used effectively during World War I. After the war, he had risen to the rank of general.

In a bombing experiment in 1921, Mitchell proved airplanes could sink any type of ship—even gigantic battleships. He wanted the government to create a powerful air force.

No one listened. Mitchell strongly criticized his superiors for neglecting airpower. Angered, the army commanders court-martialed him for insubordination, or publicly showing disrespect for senior officers. They punished him by suspending him from duty. Rather than endure the embarrassment of suspension, Mitchell resigned.

But he didn't stop campaigning for an official air force. He wrote magazine articles and gave speeches. He pleaded with the president, warning that hostile nations were building up air forces that eventually would be used against America. Mitchell predicted, correctly, that America would someday be bombarded by Japanese airplanes on a Sunday morning. That's exactly what happened at Pearl Harbor in December 1941.

The United States Air Force Is Born

As airplanes improved during the 1920s and '30s, the U.S. Army Air Corps (the old Air Service) became a big part of America's attack and defense system. In addition to planes, America and other countries were using "airships" called *dirigibles*, types of monstrous, guided balloons with motors and propellers.

By the end of World War II, the army's aerial forces had become very big and especially important to the nation's military organization. The government declared the United States Air Force to be a separate branch of service as of September 18, 1947. General Carl Spaatz was named its first commander, or chief of staff.

The USS Arizona sinks in flames following Japan's bombing of Pearl Harbor, Hawaii, in 1941. The attack led to the United States entering the war as an ally to Great Britain and the Soviet Union.

The navy, however, kept its own special air program. An aircraft carrier is a movable airport that can take its airplanes to any place in any ocean around the world. It makes sense for the navy to control not just its ships but also the airplanes and helicopters they carry.

Today's United States Air Force

The Department of the Air Force is now one of the nation's three armed forces departments. The other two are the Department of the Army and the Department of the Navy.

Our air force operates about 100 major air bases, some of them overseas.

Almost 400,000 men and women serve in the U.S. Air Force; a quarter of a million more serve in the U.S. Air Force Reserve and the U.S. Air National Guard. Counting reserve forces, the USAF has more than 6,000 aircraft. They include fighter planes like the F-16 Fighting Falcon, which can fire guided bombs—"smart bombs"—and score hits with incredible accuracy. Another new kind of weapon is the F-117A, a "stealth" plane that can avoid detection by enemy radar.

The *F* in "F-16" means the plane is among the fighter class of aircraft. Letter *B* (as in "B-1B" or "B-2") means it's a bomber. *C* (the "C-5 Galaxy" or "C-130 Hercules") signifies a cargo plane.

The designation *A* refers to an attack plane. It is similar to a fighter but is designed for a different kind of maneuvering. Craft such as the A-10 are not built primarily to fight enemy airplanes in the sky but rather to fly low and attack ground targets.

Some planes are designed not for fighting but for transporting heavy equipment (tanks and trucks) and large numbers of military personnel. Get up close to a Starlifter or Galaxy transport plane, and you will be amazed that such a mountain of machinery can fly itself, much less carry many tons of cargo!

All these planes use state-of-the-art science. Computers, both on the ground and in the air, play a major role in controlling each flight. One very special kind of airplane, the AWACS, is so advanced it is fully understood by only a few people in the air force itself. AWACS stands for Airborne Warning and Control System. It made big news in 1991 during the Persian Gulf War. It is a single, large airplane, but it also is a flying control center from which an entire military operation can be coordinated, including land, air, and sea forces. The staff inside the AWACS plane, using the most advanced equipment, collect and compare all the information being gathered about the operation— enemy troops and equipment, weather forecasts, terrain (land features), etc. Based on their findings, major military decisions are made.

Faster Than Sound

In the late 1940s, jet power began to replace propellers as the means of making airplanes move through the air. Jet planes are much faster. Some of today's USAF fighters can travel faster than the speed of sound! Just how fast is that? About 760 mph (more than 10 times the speed limit on most interstate highways). When U.S. test pilot Chuck Yeager became the first human to break the sound barrier in 1947, his "rocket plane" was shaken violently by shock waves that were building up in the air in front of him. It was very frightening, and it caused a mysterious explosion known as a "sonic boom."

Today, sonic travel is not unusual. In addition to military planes and spacecraft, even passenger airliners (namely, Concorde jets) can fly faster than sound. In fact, experimental rocket planes have gone as fast as Mach 6.72. That is 6.72 times the speed of sound, or more than 4,000

FIRST SUPERSONIC FLIGHT 1947

6062

USA 32

1997

A postage stamp depicts the flight of the Glamorous Glennis, Chuck Yeager's aircraft from his successful attempt at breaking the sound barrier. Today, most military fighter aircraft can fly well beyond the speed of sound.

mph. And amazingly, American space engineers are working on a plane that reportedly may fly at more than 17,000 mph.

Rockets and Missiles

Manned aircraft aren't the only weapons used by the USAF. In fact, the country's greatest form of airpower is not airplanes but different types of guided missiles. The U.S. Air Force controls missile units in many different locations. It is also responsible for the nation's warning and defense system to protect against enemy missiles.

Some of our missiles are short-range, accurate only at a distance of several hundred miles. Others are long-range, accurate at thousands of miles. These are known as *intercontinental ballistic missiles*, or ICBMs. *Intercontinental* means "between continents." A long-range missile can be launched from our continent (North America) and explode on a different continent far across the sea.

We think of rocketry as a fairly modern science. It actually dates back centuries, possibly to China. Robert

Goddard, America's most famous early rocket scientist, was sending up rockets powered by liquid fuel 15 years before the United States entered World War II.

Naturally, rockets and missiles entered the domain of the air force.

What Does the Air Force Do?

The U.S. Air Force has several vital tasks. It must protect the country from aerial attacks by other countries. In foreign lands in wartime, it can be used to help American soldiers carry out their assaults on the enemy. At the same time, it can protect our soldiers and sailors from opposing aircraft.

Our air force played a key role in winning the 1991 Persian Gulf War. After transporting a massive military force to the area, its bombers and other airplanes were ordered into action over Iraq, which had violated international laws by occupying neighboring Kuwait, an American ally. By the time the bombers of America and its partner nations had finished their work, Iraq could offer little resistance against American ground forces. Iraq quickly surrendered, and U.S. losses were extremely light.

Air force planes usually operate in groups. The smallest unit, called a *squadron*, consists of about 20 planes with their pilots, other airborne professionals, and ground support crews. Several squadrons may be assigned to operate together, forming a *wing*. Two or more wings can form a *division*, and several divisions make up a *command*.

As we have seen, the air force also maintains and directs our nation's guided missile system. And it operates satellites in space that are used for military observation (spying) and communications.

In peacetime, air force transport planes can be seen overhead, carrying people and cargo—often medical relief supplies—across the country and around the world. Such missions of mercy began shortly after the air force was born. In 1948–49, American, British, and French air force

A satellite is placed into Earth's orbit. The air force operates a number of satellites, which are used for gathering intelligence and communications. Many people believe that the future of the air force lies in outer space.

planes flew almost 300,000 missions to drop more than 2 million tons of food and other supplies to West Berlin, which was being cut off from the world by Soviet forces.

Sometimes, air force planes and helicopters are called in for aerial rescue operations involving civilians. And air force personnel and equipment are invaluable in helping the National Weather Service observe and track hurricanes.

Airmen and Officers

As in the U.S. Army, the highest-ranking air force officers are generals. To become a general, officers work their way through the ranks over time. Just below the rank of general is lieutenant general. Below that, in descending order of rank, are major general, brigadier general, colonel, lieutenant colonel, major, captain, first lieutenant, and the lowest, second lieutenant.

Enlisted personnel do not rise to these ranks. An air force recruit starts off as an *airman basic.* After basic training, the airman is sent to a training school to prepare for his or her special role in the air force.

The chain of rank progresses upward to airman, airman first class, sergeant or senior airman, staff sergeant, technical sergeant, master sergeant, senior master sergeant, and, finally, chief master sergeant.

Where are USAF officers trained? The army has its famous West Point, which has turned out some of the finest officers in the world since the 1800s. The navy has Annapolis. The air force, too, has a special training college, though it may be less well-known. The U.S. Air Force Academy is located near Colorado Springs, Colorado. Established in 1954, it has a student body of more than 4,000. Most of the students attend by winning appointments from their congressional representatives. They are students but also employees of the military. The government pays all their academy expenses as well as a small salary. In return, they agree to serve in the air force. They graduate as second lieutenants.

If they need further study, academy graduates may be sent to the Air Command and Staff College of Air University at Maxwell Air Force Base in Alabama. This is considered graduate school for USAF officers.

Meanwhile, many colleges and universities offer Air Force Reserve Officer Training Corps (AFROTC) programs. Students may also be admitted to the force's officer training school at Lackland Air Force Base in Texas.

American troops in landing craft go ashore on one of several beaches in Normandy, France, on D-Day, June 6, 1944. The landing was part of an all-out Allied assault on northern France, the beginning of a sweep through Europe that would finally defeat Nazi Germany.

CHAPTER 5

The Marines

THE U.S. MARINE CORPS has the reputation of being the toughest branch of our armed forces. This reputation has been won with bloody, extremely difficult achievements over a period of more than two centuries. In wartime, when U.S. troops must land and fight in enemy countries, the marines usually are the first soldiers to go in, clearing the way. "First to Fight" is the slogan the U.S. Marine Corps adopted in World War I.

But the Marine Corps is special in other ways. It is different because it does many kinds of things the other service branches do, all under one command. It has hard-trained combat soldiers—rifle-bearing infantry units are its heart and soul. It also has skilled aircraft pilots and crews. And it goes to sea like the navy.

Soldiers at Sea

The Marine Corps, which today has about 195,000 enlisted personnel and officers, is officially part of the U.S. Navy. The word *marine* means "relating to the sea." In many ways, the Marine Corps operates as a separate branch of service within the navy, but its leader, or "commandant," reports to the secretary of the navy. And if the U.S. president believes it necessary, marines can be attached to the army or can be ordered to serve in other positions. The Marine Corps has no ships of its own. Its people and airplanes are transported at sea aboard U.S. Navy vessels.

Ancient Greek and Roman marines were literally soldiers who went to sea in ships. Naval battles in those times, before gunpowder and cannons were mounted aboard warships, were fought when opposing ships drew alongside each other. While sailors struggled to control the ship's movements, marines engaged in hand-to-hand combat, striving to board and capture the enemy vessel.

As naval warfare developed, marines became the combat soldiers of the world's navies. They fight on land when ground operations are part of naval operations. They defend naval bases onshore, and as in days of old, they are available to help defend naval ships. U.S. Marines also guard American embassies and other U.S. government offices in foreign countries.

Like the U.S. Army and Navy, the country's Marine Corps dates to the Revolutionary War. Marines served with both the army and navy in different battles. A typical marine operation was to row ashore from ships and capture enemy positions on or near the coast. Although the corps was discontinued after the Revolution, a permanent Marine Corps was established in 1798.

During its first 50 years, the Marine Corps fought in places as far away as the Mediterranean Sea and Mexico. That's why "The Marines' Hymn" begins with the stirring line, "From the halls of Montezuma [Mexico City] to the shores of Tripoli [Mediterranean coast]." They later protected Americans in China during the Boxer Rebellion and in Panama before the opening of the Panama Canal.

Marines fought on land and at sea during the Civil War. They were at the forefront of fighting in the Philippines and Cuba during the Spanish-American War. In World War I, they were among the first American troops to fight in Europe. In World War II, they distinguished themselves in both Europe and the Pacific islands.

Their reputation for courage in the face of death was sealed with their amphibious (involving both land and water) landings on Japanese-held islands south of Japan in the last years of World War II. They boarded small troop-carrying craft on American ships anchored just offshore and "hit the beach," often in the face of withering enemy machine-gun fire.

American marines' most famous victory was the bloody conquest of Iwo Jima Island in 1945. It is believed to have been the greatest battle in history fought by marines alone. More than 21,000 American soldiers died before the island was secured. The bronze statue of marines raising the U.S. flag over Iwo Jima, based on a war correspondent's photograph, is one of the nation's most famous military landmarks. It can be seen at the Marine Corps War Memorial near Washington, D.C.

Marines later fought in the Korean, Vietnam, and Persian Gulf Wars.

"The Few. The Proud."

Young people between the ages of 17 and 28 can apply for the Marine Corps. Not surprisingly, basic training for applicants who are accepted into the U.S. Marine Corps is considered particularly rugged. Boot camp lasts 10 weeks. Soldiers then are sent to advanced training schools.

Marines hoist the American flag after having taken a strategic hilltop from the Japanese forces that were entrenched on the island of Iwo Jima. This image has come to symbolize the efforts and sacrifices made by the U.S. Marines.

Many Marine Corps officers are trained at the U.S. Naval Academy. They graduate as second lieutenants. The order of rank among marine officers and enlisted personnel is closely akin to that in the army—not the navy. Marine ranks range from private up to general.

The Marine Corps also draws officers from the Naval Reserve Officers Training Corps and from colleges and universities, as well as from its enlisted personnel who show special leadership capability. Officer candidates undergo lengthy training in tactics, weapons, and other subjects at the Marine Corps school in Quantico, Virginia.

Many of the ground weapons used by marines are similar to those of the army. Many of their aircraft are like

those flown by navy pilots. But marines are trained to use their weapons in special situations that call for careful teamwork between ground, air, and/or sea forces.

Interestingly, while the Marine Corps is considered an especially tough branch of the service, it also is known for—of all things—its music. One of America's greatest composers, John Philip Sousa, directed the marine band during the 1880s. Today, the United States Marine Band, known as "the President's Own," is the official military band for ceremonies of state at the White House.

The United States Marine Band performs at all events and diplomatic functions held at the White House.

The United States Coast Guard often puts itself at great risk to ensure the safety of other vessels. Here, a Coast Guard vessel braves rough seas as it patrols the U.S. coastline along the Atlantic seaboard.

CHAPTER 6

The Coast Guard and the Reserve Forces

MANY AMERICANS DON'T UNDERSTAND the difference between the United States Coast Guard and the United States Navy. There are some similarities. They both operate ships at sea. Their men and women have the same ranks. Their uniforms are somewhat similar.

During war, the Coast Guard functions as part of the navy. But in peacetime, the Coast Guard is a special military branch with a special purpose. It is not part of the U.S. Department of Defense, like the navy, army, and air force. Instead, it is controlled by the Department of Transportation.

Coastal Protection

As its name suggests, the Coast Guard protects America's seaports and coastal areas. It watches for foreign surface ships, submarines, and aircraft that might be hostile to the United States. It also is a law enforcement agency, responsible for enforcing U.S. laws at sea. For example, coast guard vessels often are involved in capturing boats used for drug smuggling.

Most notable among the Coast Guard's varied tasks in peacetime is water safety and rescue. Coast Guard crews can board and inspect civilian craft to make sure they are seaworthy. When planes crash into the sea or ships find themselves sinking or otherwise in distress near shore, the Coast Guard is quickly at the scene.

A Long Tradition of Coastal Defense

America created its Coast Guard in 1790, several years after the War of Independence. At first it was called the Revenue Marine, then the Revenue Cutter Service. It became known as the Coast Guard in 1915. Its main task in the early years was to prevent smuggling—illegally bringing goods into or transporting them out of the country. This remains one of its duties, particularly in the war against drugs.

Two of its most important roles now are to enforce fishing laws within 200 miles of U.S. shores and to operate the International Ice Patrol in North Atlantic waters. The ice patrol, which was begun largely as a result of the *Titanic* disaster, monitors seasonal floes of dangerous ice fields and bergs floating southward from the polar ice cap. The U.S. Coast Guard also operates icebreakers, ships that make way for American ships in the frigid waters near the North and South Poles, off the shores of Alaska, and in the freshwater Great Lakes.

The Coast Guard also operates the nation's lighthouses, buoys, and other navigation aids. And it must prevent and investigate pollution in U.S. waters. Pollution is caused by illegal dumping at sea and by shipping accidents. One of the worst pollution-causing American maritime accidents on record occurred at sea when the *Exxon Valdez* ran aground off the coast of Alaska in 1989.

Its hull was punctured, and more than 10 million gallons of oil marred the waters and beaches, killed thousands of animals, and seriously affected the fishing industry.

The United States Coast Guard vessel Polar Star *breaks a route through the ice pack off the coast of Antarctica. Coast Guard icebreakers also routinely create routes for shipping through many of America's waterways when the cold of winter makes them almost impassable.*

A Small, Well-Trained Service

About 45,000 sailors, officers, and civilian workers make up the U.S. Coast Guard in peacetime. That's a small force, compared to the navy or army. They operate not only ships but rescue and surveillance helicopters and special-purpose airplanes too.

The Coast Guard Academy, founded in 1876, is in New London, Connecticut. It has a small enrollment—fewer than a thousand students—and accepts student applicants based on competition, not on appointments by senators or congressional representatives.

America's First Militias

Even before the American Revolution (which began in 1775), **militia** units were in force on the new continent. Each colony frequently called out bands of armed citizens to fight hostile natives. During the Revolutionary

War, many able-bodied colonial men who supported the patriot cause didn't join the militia because they wanted to; they *had* to. Each colony was required to raise, organize, and train its own militia force.

But George Washington and other revolutionary commanders had a problem in relying on the colonial militia. Many of the militiamen fought to defend their separate colonies, not the country as a whole. When the British threatened their homes directly, the militia soldiers fought valiantly. When the immediate threat was over, they expected to go home to their families. They were not inclined to march dozens or hundreds of miles to fight in other battles two or three colonies away.

Yet the colonial militia units were vital in helping America win its independence. After the Revolution, the young country and its individual states continued to call out local militias in times of crisis.

"The Guard"

Probably the best-known reserve force is our Army National Guard. Actually, the National Guard is as old as the country. During the American Revolution, all 13 colonies trained militia companies. As previously discussed, these were not professional (full-time) soldiers. Rather, they were average citizens from all walks of life who banded together to protect their homes and families, as well as their colony as a whole.

After the Revolution, when the colonies began to expand and divide into states, all free men from ages 18 to 45 in America were considered members of their state militias. They could be "called up" to fight in times of trouble. Basically, that explains what the Army National Guard (usually referred to as simply "the National Guard") does today. Every state in America has a separate National Guard. But not every able-bodied adult is automatically a member of it.

An Air National Guard A-10 Thunderbolt takes off during a training exercise. The Air National Guard patrols United States airspace and is often called into active duty during conflicts.

Enlistment in a state's National Guard is voluntary. Men and women who enlist undergo basic training like army soldiers. But afterward, they do not serve full-time in the army. They live at home and hold ordinary civilian jobs in their hometowns.

To stay in training, they report for duty one weekend each month at their local National Guard armory. For two weeks in the summer, they participate in special training exercises. Those are their only service obligations—unless an emergency arises. At any time of year, they may be summoned on short notice to, for example, keep order and direct traffic in disaster zones.

The country also is served by Air National Guard units, consisting of pilots, crews, and support staff.

Other Reserves

The Army Reserve is a similar organization. Enlistees undergo basic and advanced army training, then go home to work as civilians. They report regularly for exercises and training. But the Army Reserve is not attached to any state. It is under the direct command of the U.S. Army.

Other branches of our armed forces also keep reserve units. The Naval Reserve is made up of officers and enlisted personnel who undergo both basic and advanced training, just like members of the regular navy. After training, though, they return to civilian life. Like members of the Army National Guard, they stay in training by drilling one weekend a month and reporting for active duty two weeks a year.

The air force, like the other main military branches, has a reserve body of men and women. The Marine Corps also has reserve units. After basic and advanced training, members lead civilian lives and report for duty one weekend a month and two weeks a year.

Answering the Patriotic Call

It's interesting that many of the men and women who presently participate in our reserve forces are **veterans** of regular service. Our military leaders are eager to persuade these individuals to join the reserves because they are not just fully trained but are disciplined and have valuable military experience.

And reserve service is appealing to countless soldiers, sailors, and fliers after they complete their regular tours of duty. The pay and benefits are excellent, and the veterans feel well qualified to perform their jobs in the reserves. At the same time, it offers them a way to continue serving their country after they return to civilian life.

Glossary

Allies—Countries or individuals fighting on the same side in a conflict. During the world wars, the United States and its partner nations became known formally as the Allies.

Arsenal—A nation's or military force's collection of weapons.

Artillery—Heavy field weapons such as cannons and, in today's armies, rockets.

Cavalry—Mounted or "mobile" soldiers. In ages past, cavalry referred to fighters mounted on horseback. Today, tank and helicopter units are also called cavalry because they can take their firepower quickly from one place to another.

Civilian—An ordinary citizen, as distinguished from a person serving in the military. "Civilian clothes" are ordinary or "plain" clothes, not uniforms.

Defense—A nation's system of weapons, ships, planes, and other fighting machines and the men and women who operate and support them.

Militia—Citizens (as distinguished from professional or "regular" soldiers) who are called out on short notice for defense when their communities are threatened.

Recruiting—Enlisting individuals to join a branch of the service. A recruit is a person who has just joined a branch of the armed forces and is undergoing basic training.

Veteran—In military usage, a man or woman who has served in any branch of the armed forces.

Further Reading

Green, Michael. *Serving Your Country: The United States Army.* Mankato, MN: Capstone Press, 1998.

————. *Serving Your Country: The United States Navy.* Mankato, MN: Capstone Press, 1998.

Halasz, Robert. *The U.S. Marines.* Brookfield, CT: The Millbrook Press, 1993.

Hough, Richard. *A History of Fighting Ships.* London: Octopus Books Limited, 1975.

Hughes, Libby. *West Point.* New York: Dillon Press, 1993.

Moran, Tom. *The U.S. Army.* Minneapolis, MN: Lerner Publications Company, 1990.

Naden, Corinne J., and Rose Blue. *The U.S. Navy.* Brookfield, CT: The Millbrook Press, 1993.

Rhea, John. *The Department of the Air Force.* New York: Chelsea House Publishers, 1990.

Warner, J. F. *The U.S. Marine Corps.* Minneapolis, MN: Lerner Publications Company, 1991.

Index

ABOUT THE AUTHOR: Daniel E. Harmon is the author of 18 nonfiction books on topics ranging from history to humor. He also is the editor of *The Lawyer's PC*, a national technology newsletter, and associate editor/art director of *Sandlapper: The Magazine of South Carolina*. Harmon lives in Spartanburg, SC.

SENIOR CONSULTING EDITOR Arthur M. Schlesinger, jr. is the leading American historian of our time. He won the Pulitzer Prize for his book *The Age of Jackson* (1945) and again for *A Thousand Days* (1965). This chronicle of the Kennedy Administration also won a National Book Award. Professor Schlesinger is the Albert Schweitzer Professor of the Humanities at the City University of New York, and he has been involved in several other Chelsea House projects, including the REVOLUTIONARY WAR LEADERS and COLONIAL LEADERS series.

Picture Credits

page

8: Morton Beebe, S.F./ Corbis
10: Aero Graphics, Inc./ Corbis
12: Araldo de Luca/Corbis
19: Annie Griffiths Belt/ Corbis
22: Corbis
24: AP/Wide World Photos
27: Archive Photos
28: Archive Photos

32: AP/Wide World Photos
34: Aero Graphics Inc./ Corbis
36: AFP/Corbis
41: Bettmann/Corbis
44: AP/Wide World Photos
46: NASA/Roger Ressmeyer/Corbis
48: Hulton Deutsch Collection/Corbis
52: AP/Wide World Photos

53: AP/Wide World Photos
54: Jim Sugar Photography/Corbis
57: James L. Amos/Corbis
59: John H. Clark/Corbis